Proofreading &
Grammar Drills
Workbook

D1611454

Ashan R. Hampton

Cornerstone Publishing
Arkansas

Published by Cornerstone Communications & Publishing, Little Rock, Arkansas.

Cover Design: Ashan R. Hampton
Cover photo: © Can Stock Photo/3d_vicka; HiClipart
Interior photos: © Can Stock Photo/yupiramos, scanrail, nmarques74, ggraphstudio; Pexels, Andrea Piacquadio

Websites: www.arhampton.com
www.prowritingskills.com

Library of Congress Control Number: 2020915914
ISBN-13: 978-1-71664-564-8

Cataloging-in-Publication Data is on file with the Library of Congress.

10 9 8 7 6 5 4 3 2 1

Pro Writing Skills Academy
Online Writing Classes

www.prowritingskills.com

Beyond Basic Grammar

Business Grammar Essentials

Core Grammar Essentials

Grammar Essentials Jump-start

Grant Writing Essentials

Proofreading Power

Public Speaking Skills

Smarty Pants Vocabulary Builders

www.arhampton.com

About the Author

Ashan R. Hampton has worked as an English instructor in higher education for over 20 years, most notably at Morehouse College in Atlanta, Georgia. She is also a proud graduate of the *Donaghey Scholars Program* at the University of Arkansas at Little Rock under the direction of Dr. C. Earl Ramsey, Emeritus.

Ashan's original research, *History of the Arkansas State Hospital 1859-1930*, was published in the *Pulaski County Historical Review* (1995), and continues to be cited by history scholars today. Her articles on notable African American Arkansans also appear in the *Encyclopedia of Arkansas History and Culture*.

With her doctoral studies on hold, Ashan has found success in online education. She produces and teaches her own writing and grammar courses for global audiences through her company, Cornerstone Communications & Publishing. Ashan is also a published author, digital media producer, proofreader and copyeditor.

Visit her website: **www.arhampton.com**.

About this Book

This workbook only provides exercises and answers. No explanations for why an answer is correct or not are given. For that level of instruction, you should have already taken the *Core Grammar Essentials, Business Grammar Essentials, Workplace Grammar & Style and Proofreading Power* online classes. Before this book, you should have already worked through *"Grammar Essentials for Proofreading, Copyediting and Business Writing"* and *"Proofreading Power Skills & Drills"*. As the third book in this series, all of the exercises in this book stem from the instruction provided in the online courses and books listed above.

In order to get the most out of this book, you need intermediate to advanced grammar, usage, punctuation and writing skills. If you need a refresher, please take the online classes above or purchase the grammar books. In order to fix errors, you must be able to identify them, which is the focus of the grammar courses.

Good writing begins with good grammar. Effective proofreaders need to be good writers. So, if you find yourself getting stuck on some of the exercises, or if you need additional explanations for the concepts presented in this book, please take time for a comprehensive grammar and proofreading review with the previously mentioned online and print book resources.

For more information on the above resources, click "Books" at
www.arhampton.com.

Contents

Exercise Directions

In the majority of the exercises, your task is to **find and correct all errors**. Therefore, directions do not appear on every exercise. In addition to text errors, you should also pay attention to formatting issues, such as line spacing and font size. However, there are no extra space errors between characters, but full paragraph justification might make it appear so.

In fact, pages 32 and 46 in the book *"Proofreading Power Skills & Drills: Become an Effective Proofreader"* list the types of errors you should look for when you sit down to proofread a document—or in this case—to complete these exercises. For your convenience, those checklists have been included below and on the next page.

One more thing, the exercises reflect a variety of everyday writing styles. Nothing is incorrect due to personal style preferences, so do not attempt to rewrite the passages.

The grammar exercises are pretty self-explanatory. If no directions are given, circle the correct answer or fill in the blank. Remember, these exercises are geared toward people who already work as proofreaders or editors, and those with intermediate to advanced writing skills. If you find yourself struggling, go back and review the online classes and books previously mentioned under the "About this Book" section on page 6.

What Do Proofreaders Check?

- Capitalization
- Formatting
- Grammar
- Mechanics
- Numbers
- Punctuation
- Spelling and usage
- Visual images

Proofreading Checklist

See the full list on the next page.

Proofreading Checklist for Error Correction

First Review: Check Formatting

- Headings, subheadings and headlines
- Headers and footers
- Page numbers
- Font style and font size
- Spacing: between sentences, words, and around the page
- Chapter titles, book titles, article titles, author names
- Alignment: paragraphs, bullet points, numbered or alphabetical lists
- Legal or other disclaimers; copyright statements
- **Table of contents:** page numbers in TOC match chapter pages
- **Index:** consistently use lowercase or title case; page numbers for index entries match their location in the document text.

Second Review: Images & Graphics

- Photographs
- Illustrations/cartoons
- Company/business logos
- Graphics: charts and tables
- Captions: text and alignment; accurately identifies image
- Image clarity and readability
- Wording on or around images: typos or misspellings

Third Review: Body Text

- Grammar errors
- Spelling errors
- Typos; missing words
- Numbers, proper names, telephone numbers

Everyday Proofreading #1

I just read a Time magazine article about Bono, the leader singer of the irish rock band U2. I really admire him because he's not only talentid but also worked hard on charitable causes. He is especialy interested in helping the people of africa. Most rock stars are selfish and self-centered, but he's making it cool to care.

Answers: Everyday Proofreading #1

I just read a ***Time*** magazine article about Bono, the **lead** singer of the **Irish** rock band U2. I really admire him because he's not only **talented,** but also **works** hard on charitable causes. He is **especially** interested in helping the people of **Africa**. Most rock stars are selfish and self-centered, but he's making it cool to care.

Ashan R. Hampton

13

Everyday Proofreading #2

I get so anoyed by people who drive SUVs. Most of the time, you see just one or too people in a huge vehicle that seats seven or none people. Motorists in these vehicles wasting gas could be driving more fuel-efficient cars and helping to make oil supplies last longer. Its aggravating to try to see around them. Thay completely block the view of people in cars: that's unsafe. When I try to make a right turn and one pulls up beside me, I can't see oncoming trafic any more. Roads less safe with SUV's on them. In accidents, the people who get injured or killed are the ones in the core not the suv.

Answers: Everyday Proofreading #2

I get so **annoyed** by people who drive SUVs. Most of the time, you see just one or **two** people in a huge vehicle that seats seven or **nine** people. Motorists in these vehicles wasting gas could be driving more fuel-efficient cars and helping to make oil supplies last longer. **It's** aggravating to try to see around them. **They** completely block the view of people in cars**;** that's unsafe. When I try to make a right turn and one pulls up beside me, I can't see oncoming **traffic anymore**. Roads **are** less safe with **SUVs** on them. In accidents, the people who get injured or killed are the ones in the **car,** not the **SUV**.

Everyday Proofreading #3

Realty TV Shows

Who.	Ordinary people become famous; Mark Burnett produces many of the best shows, Donald Trump, Simon Cowell
What?	*American Idol, Survivor, The Apprentice, Big Brother, The Amazing Race*—has won awards
Where!	New York and other big cities, tropical islands
When?	All the time—there"s always one on TV!
Why?	Vuers can't get enough; participants want a chance to win big money, become famous, get into showbiz
How?	Series taped in secret locations, broadcast a few months later, but some (like *Big Brother*) are broadcast live

Answers: Everyday Proofreading #3

<u>Reality</u> TV Shows

Who<u>?</u>	Ordinary people become famous; Mark Burnett produces many of the best shows, Donald Trump, Simon Cowell
What?	*American Idol, Survivor, The Apprentice, Big Brother, The Amazing Race*—has won awards
Where<u>?</u>	New York and other big cities, tropical islands
When?	All the time—<u>**there's**</u> always one on TV!
Why?	<u>**Viewers**</u> can't get enough; participants want a chance to win big money, become famous, get into showbiz
How?	Series taped in secret locations, broadcast a few months later, but some (like *Big Brother*) are broadcast live

Everyday Proofreading #4

Annie oakley was one of the best sharpshooters of all time. From 1869 to 1875, as a poor child in Ohio, Annie pays off the family's mortgage by hunting and selling wild game. In her teens, she competed against Frank Butler, a famous marksman who came to town, and beat him by 1 point european kings and queens loved to watch her perform, and she once shod a cigarette from the lips of the future Kaiser Wilhelm 2 of Germany. Years later Annie married Butler and joined the Wild Bill's Wild West Show where she was the star.

Answers: Everyday Proofreading #4

Annie **Oakley** was one of the best sharpshooters of all time. From 1869 to 1875, as a poor child in Ohio, Annie **paid** off the family's mortgage by hunting and selling wild game. In her teens, she competed against Frank Butler, a famous marksman who came to town, and beat him by **one** point**.** **European** kings and queens loved to watch her perform, and she once **shot** a cigarette from the lips of the future Kaiser Wilhelm **II** of Germany. Years later**,** Annie married Butler and joined the ***Wild Bill's Wild West Show*** where she was the star.

Everyday Proofreading #5

Online Etiquete

In recent years, the concept of online etiquette, often referred to as *netiquette*, has evolved with the rise of the internet as a primary source of commmunication. Just as there are prescribed rules of social conduct for voice communication, or when people sit down to eat a meal together, there are similar social expectations of how individuals should behave when they communicate over the Internet, by email, or face-to-face with other learners and they're instructor in a classroom.

Answers: Everyday Proofreading #5

Online <u>Etiquette</u>

In recent years, the concept of online etiquette, often referred to as *netiquette*, has evolved with the rise of the internet as a primary source of **communication**. Just as there are prescribed rules of social conduct for voice communication, or when people sit down to eat a meal together, there are similar social expectations of how individuals should behave when they communicate over the **internet**, by email, or face-to-face with other learners and **their** instructor in a classroom.

Everyday Proofreading #6

(1) At Paradice Produce, attractive displays of fruit and vegetables caught my eye. (2) On the left, oranges, lemons, and apples were stacked in neat pyramids. (c) In the center of the store, baskets of ripe peaches, plums, and raspberries were grouped in a kind of steel life. (4) Many nutritionists believe that berries help prevent certain diseases. (5) On the right, the leafy green vegetables had been arranged according to intensity of color: dark green spinach, then romaine lettuce and parsley; next the lighter iceberg lettuce, and finally the nearly white chinese cabbage. (5) On the wall above the greens hunged braided ropes of garlic.

Answers: Everyday Proofreading #6

(1) At **<u>Paradise</u>** Produce, attractive displays of fruit and vegetables caught my eye. (2) On the left, oranges, lemons, and apples were stacked in neat pyramids. **<u>(3)</u>** In the center of the store, baskets of ripe peaches, plums, and raspberries were grouped in a kind of **<u>still</u>** life. **(4) Many nutritionists believe that berries help prevent certain diseases.** (5) On the right, the leafy green vegetables had been arranged according to intensity of color: dark green spinach, then romaine lettuce and parsley; next the lighter iceberg lettuce, and finally the nearly white **<u>Chinese</u>** cabbage. **<u>(6)</u>** On the wall above the greens **<u>hung</u>** braided ropes of garlic.

Everyday Proofreading #7

John Bush (1856–1916)

John Edward Bush, a chairman of the Republican Party in Arkansas, rose from poverty to national prominence when he co-founded the Mosaic Templars of America (MTA), an African-American fraternal organization of international scope, spanning twenty-six states and six foreign countries from the 1880s until the 1930s.

Headquartered in Little Rock (Pulaski County), MTA became one of the largest and most successful black-owned business enterprises in the nation and the world; it included an ensurance company, a building and loan association, a hospital, a business college, a publishing house, and a nursing school. Living most of his early life in the downtown 9th Street district of Little Rock, Bush was widely acknowledged as one of the wealthiest black men in Arkansas and a progenitor of the economic development and progress of black American entrepreneurs.

John Bush was born a slave on November 14 1856 in Moscow Tennessee. In 1862, Bush and his mother and sister were brought to Arkansas by their owner, who was trying to stay ahead of Union troops. His mother was Mary E. Cobb, and his sister was Mollie Bush Henderson, mother of Arkansas's first black jeweler, J. E. Henderson. Bush and his family were free at the end of the Civil War, but his mother died shortly after their arrival in Little Rock. He often had to sleep under bridges or in stables or deserted houses. He frequently lived off the kindness of strangers but performed odd jobs suited to children, such as running errands, watering stock, or washing dishes to earn his keep. One day, while Bush was throwing rocks, a man named Colonel R. C. Lacy saw him and carried him by force to school. However, Bush liked school and studied late at night as he was often unable to attend during the day.

Photo Curtesy of the Butler Center for Arkansas Studies, Central Arkansas Libary System

Answers: Everyday Proofreading #7

John Bush (1856–1916)

John Edward Bush, a chairman of the Republican Party in Arkansas, rose from poverty to national prominence when he co-founded the Mosaic Templars of America (MTA), an African-American fraternal organization of international scope, spanning twenty-six states and six foreign countries from the 1880s until the 1930s.

Headquartered in Little Rock (Pulaski County), MTA became one of the largest and most successful black-owned business enterprises in the nation and the world; it included an **insurance** company, a building and loan association, a hospital, a business college, a publishing house, and a nursing school. Living most of his early life in the downtown 9th Street district of Little Rock, Bush was widely acknowledged as one of the wealthiest black men in Arkansas and a progenitor of the economic development and progress of black American entrepreneurs.

John Bush was born a slave on **November 14, 1856, in Moscow,** Tennessee. In 1862, Bush and his mother and sister were brought to Arkansas by their owner, who was trying to stay ahead of Union troops. His mother was Mary E. Cobb, and his sister was Mollie Bush Henderson, mother of Arkansas's first black jeweler, J. E. Henderson. Bush and his family were **freed** at the end of the Civil War, but his mother died shortly after their arrival in Little Rock. Bush often had to sleep under bridges or in stables or deserted houses. He frequently lived off the kindness of strangers, but performed odd jobs suited to children, such as running errands, watering stock, or washing dishes to earn his keep. One day, while Bush was throwing rocks, a man named Colonel R. C. Lacy saw him and carried him by force to school. However, Bush liked school and studied late at night as he was often unable to attend during the day.

*Photo **Courtesy** of the Butler Center for Arkansas Studies, Central Arkansas **Library** System*

Everyday Proofreading #8

You should join the Army National Guard for several reasons. For one thing, joining is a cheap way to get in shape. Not only is physical training free, but you actually get payed to do it! Also, being an Army Natnal Guard member is interesting and action-packed. You'll get hands-on training in 1 or more of 100s of exciting specialties. You'll get opportunities to increase your knowledge of fields like mechanics, law enforcement, computers, and communications.

Along the weigh, you'll met new people who share your desire for adventure, and you'll form friendships that will last a lifetime. If you join the Guard, you will also learn leadership skills that you can use in your own community, and in times of crisis when you'll be called to action to perform rescue missions and help victims of dissasters. By helping your fellow americans, you'll be serving your country. In fact, that's the most important reason of all. Join the Army National Guard. We can't defend this country without you!

Answers: Everyday Proofreading #8

You should join the Army National Guard for several reasons. For one thing, joining is a cheap way to get in shape. Not only is physical training free, but you actually get **paid** to do it! Also, being an Army **National** Guard member is interesting and action-packed. You'll get hands-on training in **one** or more of **hundreds** of exciting specialties. **You'll get opportunities to increase your knowledge of fields like mechanics, law enforcement, computers, and communications.** <--------(Change Font)

Along the **way**, you'll **meet** new people who share your desire for adventure, and you'll form friendships that will last a lifetime. If you join the **Army National** Guard, you will also learn leadership skills that you can use in your own community, and in times of crisis when you'll be called to action to perform rescue missions and help victims of **disasters**. By helping your fellow **A**mericans, you'll be serving your country. In fact, that's the most important reason of all. Join the Army National Guard. We can't defend this country without you!

Everyday Proofreading #9

Some seemingly harmless substances can innerfear with the way medicines work inside the body. Take grapefruit juice, for example. it disrupts the action of enzymes that brake down drugs in the smalll intestine before they are absorbed into the bloodstreem. Therefore, taking a medication with gradefruit juice may cause the drug to enter the blood in dangerously high concentrations. If this happens, not only is the drug less effective, but serious side effects can result. Many common medacations, including antidepressants, antihistamines, and cholesterol drugs are negatively effected by grapefruit juice.

Answers: Everyday Proofreading #9

Some seemingly harmless substances can **interfere** with the way medicines work inside the body. Take grapefruit juice, for example. **It** disrupts the action of enzymes that **break** down drugs in the **small** intestine before they are absorbed into the **bloodstream**. Therefore, taking a medication with **grapefruit** juice may cause the drug to enter the blood in dangerously high concentrations. If this **happens**, not only is the drug less effective, but serious side effects can result. Many common **medications**, including antidepressants, antihistamines, and cholesterol drugs are negatively **affected** by grapefruit juice.

Everyday Proofreading #10

(1) One of the most terrible encounters between sharks and humans in modern times occured during *World War* 2. (2) On July 30 1945 the Navy ship USS Indianapolis was torpedoed by a japanese submarine while sitting in the philippine sea. (3) About three hundred crewmembers were killed in the explosion. (4) 12 minutes later, the *Indianapolis* sunk, tossing the nine-hundred remaining sailors into the ocean. (e) Due to a misunderstanding, their ship was not reported missing. (f) Floating in the sea without lifeboats, the survivors began to be hounded by 100's of sharks. (g) For fore days, they had no protection against the predators. (8) Finally, on August 2nd, the men were spotted by the pilot of a patrole plane, who radioed for help. (9) Too days later, rescuers were only able to find three hundred nineteen men alive.

Answers: Everyday Proofreading #10

(1) One of the most terrible encounters between sharks and humans in modern times **occurred** during **World War** **II**. (2) On July 30**,** 1945**,** the Navy ship ***USS Indianapolis*** was torpedoed by a **Japanese** submarine while sitting in the **Philippine** **Sea**. (3) About **300** crewmembers were killed in the explosion. (4) **Twelve** minutes later, the **_USS_** *Indianapolis* sunk, tossing the **900** remaining sailors into the ocean. **(5)** Due to a misunderstanding, their ship was not reported missing. **(6)** Floating in the sea without lifeboats, the survivors began to be hounded by **hundreds** of sharks. **(7)** For **four** days, they had no protection against the predators. (8) Finally, on August **2**, the men were spotted by the pilot of a **patrol** plane, who radioed for help. (9) **Two** days later, rescuers were only able to find **319** men alive.

Everyday Proofreading #11

One look at my dog reveals that she has a mixed background. Her long, tapered nose is like those of german shepherds or Collies. On either side of her black head are small, folded-over ears like those of a Terrier. She loves to run outside with my kids. The fir around her neck is soft and thick, but on her back, it's short like a dachshund's. All over her body, her white coat is covered with black spots. Some are large, like a Beagle's, and some are very small and close together, like the spots on a dalmatian. Her tell is long and hairy, just like a Golden Retriever's.

Answers: Everyday Proofreading #11

One look at my dog reveals that she has a mixed background. Her long, tapered nose is like those of **German** shepherds or **collies**. On either side of her black head are small, folded-over ears like those of a **terrier**. ~~She loves to run outside with my kids.~~ The **fur** around her neck is soft and thick, but on her back, it's short like a dachshund's. All over her body, her white coat is covered with black spots. Some are large, like a **beagle's**, and some are very small and close together, like the spots on a dalmatian. Her **tail** is long and hairy, just like a **g**olden **r**etriever's.

NOTE:** Check the Merriam Webster's dictionary for capitalizing names of dogs.

Everyday Proofreading #12

Imagine that you are sitting in a restaurant quitely having a meal when suddenly a man nearby starts choking on a piece of food lodged in his throat. By using the heimlich maneuver, you may be able to save this person's life. Your to hands are all you need to perform this life saving technique. First, position yourself behind the choking person. Next, wrap your arms around the person's midsection, being careful not to apply any pressure to the chest or stomach. Once you're arms are around the victim, clench one hand into a fist and cup this fist in the other hand. Now turn the fist so that the clenched thumb points toward the spot between the choker's navel and midsection. Finaly, thrust inward at this spot using a quick, sharp motion. If this motion does not dislodge the food, repeat it it until the victim can breathe freely.

Answers: Everyday Proofreading #12

Imagine that you are sitting in a restaurant **quietly** having a meal when suddenly a man nearby starts choking on a piece of food lodged in his throat. By using the **Heimlich** maneuver, you may be able to save this person's life. Your **two** hands are all you need to perform this **lifesaving** technique. First, position yourself behind the choking person. Next, wrap your arms around the person's midsection, being careful not to apply any pressure to the chest or stomach. Once **your** arms are around the victim, clench one hand into a fist and cup this fist in the other hand. Now turn the fist so that the clenched thumb points toward the spot between the choker's navel and midsection. **Finally,** thrust inward at this spot using a quick, sharp motion. If this motion does not dislodge the food, repeat **it** until the victim can breathe freely.

Everyday Proofreading #13

'*Ambivalence*' can be defined as a felling or attitude that is both positive and negative at the same time. For instance, a young woman might feel ambivalent about mother-hood. She may want to have a child yet fear that motherhood will use up energy she would like to spend on her career. Or a Michigan man who is offered a slightly higher salary. In Arizona might be ambivalent about moving. He and his family don't want to leave their friends, their schools, and a city they love. On the other hand, their tempted by a larger income, Arizona"s warm climate, and clean heir. Finally, too people may have ambivalent feelings about each other, loving and dislikking each other at the same time. It hurt to be together, and it hurt to be a part... neither situation makes them happy. As these examples show, the doubble tug of ambivalence can complicate decision making.

Answers: Everyday Proofreading #13

Ambivalence can be defined as a **feeling** or attitude that is both positive and negative at the same time. For instance, a young woman might feel ambivalent about **motherhood**. She may want to have a child yet fear that motherhood will use up energy she would like to spend on her career. ~~Or~~ **A** Michigan man who is offered a slightly higher **salary in** Arizona might be ambivalent about moving. He and his family don't want to leave their friends, their schools, and a city they love. On the other hand, **they are** (they're) tempted by a larger income, **Arizona's** warm climate, and clean **air**. Finally, **two** people may have ambivalent feelings about each other, loving and **disliking** each other at the same time. It **hurts** to be together, and it **hurts** to be **apart;** neither situation makes them happy. As these examples show, the **double** tug of ambivalence can complicate decision making.

NOTE: Deleting "Or" counts as one error. Capitalizing "A" counts as a separate error. Deleting the period behind "salary" counts as one error. Lowercasing "in" counts as a separate error that needs to be corrected. The contraction "they're" is also acceptable for replacing "their". Also, correcting "apart" and adding a semicolon after it count as two separate errors.

Everyday Proofreading #14

Cold vs. Flu

Phodo by Andrea Piacquadio from Pexels

Both a cold and the flu can make you miserable, but they are different in several ways. Experts say a cold will go away by itself. However, the flu can lead to newmonia and other serious or even deadly problems. A cold usually comes on gradualy, accompanied by litttle or no fever. In contrast, the flu comes on suddenly, and its fever can spike as high as 104 degrees and linger for 3 or 4 days. Someone with a cold might experience mild body aches and fatigue, but the flew often brings severe body aches, deep fatigue, chills, and a major headache. In general, a cold is wet, with much congestion, a runny nose, and even runny eyes. The flu, on the other hand, is far dryer, marked by a dry cough.

Answers: Everyday Proofreading #14

Cold vs. Flu

<u>Photo</u> by Andrea Piacquadio from *Pexels*

Both a cold and the flu can make you miserable, but they are different in several ways. Experts say a cold will go away by itself. However, the flu can lead to **pneumonia** and other serious or even deadly problems. A cold usually comes on **gradually**, accompanied by **little** or no fever. In contrast, the flu comes on suddenly, and its fever can spike as high as 104 degrees and linger for **three** or **four** days. Someone with a cold might experience mild body aches and fatigue, but the **flu** often brings severe body aches, deep fatigue, chills, and a major headache. In general, a cold is wet, with much congestion, a runny nose, and even runny eyes. The flu, on the other hand, is far **drier**, marked by a dry cough.

Everyday Proofreading #15

As several school districts have found, moving the start time for high schools to later in the morning has several beneficial effects. One result is better school attendance. When seven Mineeapolis high schools pushed back their start times, attendance in all grades improved, and academic performance improved slightly. Another positive effect is happier students and parents. When students get more sleep, they tend to be in a bettter mood, which improves relationships with their family members. A third important outcome is an improvement in safety. When unsupervised teens get out of school later in the afternoon, they have less time to get into trouble before adults get home. Plus, there less prone to fatigue-related car accidents on their way to school in the morning.

Answers: Everyday Proofreading #15

As several school districts have found, moving the start time for high schools to later in the morning has several beneficial effects. One result is better school attendance. When seven **Minneapolis** high schools pushed back their start times, attendance in all grades improved, and academic performance improved slightly. Another positive effect is happier students and parents. When students get more sleep, they tend to be in a **better** mood, which improves relationships with their family members. A third important outcome is an improvement in safety. When unsupervised teens get out of school later in the afternoon, they have less time to get into trouble before adults get home. Plus, **they are (they're)** less prone to fatigue-related car accidents on their way to school in the morning.

Everyday Proofreading #16

The Camtrex Corporation should provide day care for the children of its employees. First of all, Collins Corporation workers need such a program. According to the Human Resources Director, about eight hundred fifty employees with small children have spouses who also work outside the home. For these workers, day care is a constant problem. Secondly, the company would undoubtedly benefit from on-site day care since workers could concentrate more fully on their jobs, secure in the knowledge that their children are nearby and well cared for. A child care program that benefits both employees and management just makes good sense.

Answers: Everyday Proofreading #16

The Camtrex Corporation should provide day care for the children of its employees. First of all, **Camtrex** Corporation workers need such a program. According to the **human resources director**, about **850** employees with small children have spouses who also work outside the home. For these workers, day care is a constant problem. **Second**, the company would undoubtedly benefit from on-site day care since workers could concentrate more fully on their jobs, secure in the knowledge that their children are nearby and well cared for. **A child care program that benefits both employees and management just makes good sense.** <----- **(Change Font)**

Proofreading Everyday Business Documents

Find errors. Correct errors.

Essential Online Classes

Core Grammar Essentials
www.arhampton.com/classes

Business Grammar Essentials
www.arhampton.com/classes

Proofreading Power
www.arhampton.com/classes

Agenda

Zoe Dane Cosmetics Agenda

Regional Meeting
Thursday, February 20th, 2020
8:30 a.m. – 1:00 p.m.
The Landscape Hotel Ballroom
Rock City, Arkansas

- Continental Breakfast
- Introduction and Welcome
  - New Product Line Overview
  - New Product Line Demonstrations
- Sales Techniques
- Department Reports

Lunch
11 a.m.-12:15 p.m.

- Report of the President   Jan Dyer
- Report of the Regional Director   Michael Stone
- Informle Q & A   Amy Dyson, Moderator
- Meeting Wrap-up   Jan Dyer
- Dismissal   Linda Eason

Aditional Information:

- Starting May 15th, seasonal store demonstrators will be hired through the Next Job Staffing Agency.

- The next regional meeting will be held in Kansas City, Missouri, April 3rd. Location TBA.

Answers: Agenda

Zoe Dane Cosmetics
Agenda

Regional Meeting
Thursday, February **20,** 2020
8:30 a.m. – 1:00 p.m.
The Landscape Hotel Ballroom
Rock City, Arkansas

- Continental Breakfast
- Introduction and Welcome
- **New Product Line Overview**   **Bullets**
- **New Product Line Demonstrations**
- Sales Techniques
- Department Reports

Lunch
11 a.m.-12:15 p.m.

• Report of the President	Jan Dyer
• Report of the Regional Director	Michael Stone
• **Informal** Q & A	Amy Dyson, Moderator
• Meeting Wrap-up	Jan Dyer
• Dismissal	Linda Eason

Additional Information:

- Starting **May 15**, seasonal store demonstrators will be hired through the Next Job Staffing Agency.

- The next regional meeting will be held in Kansas City, Missouri, April **3**. Location TBA.

Biography

Bioography
Zephyr L. Austin

Zephyr E. Austin is the Social Media Marketing Manager for Alston-Hill Marketing Agency in Columbia, South Carolina. After graduating college with a Bachelor's in english, Zephyr worked as a freelance digital marketer for local restaurants before landing a position as a website copywriter at Alston-Hill. To further enhance and legitimize her self-taught digital media skills, Zephyr earned a masters in Digital Marketing from Southern New Hampshire University. Although Zephyr loves the creative aspects of writing, web design and video production, she loves to help small business customers launch successful social media campaigns.

In 2016, Zephyr won south carolina's chamber of commerce's award for best digital media professional. Her blog articles on social media marketing have been featured on *Forbes*, The Huffington Post, and various other high-profile outlets. Her popular online classes and workshops are also well attended. Outside of work, Zephyr enjoys latin dance classes, volunteeering at a local animal shelter, and hosting dinner parties for friends and family.

Answers: Biography

Biography
Zephyr L. Austin

Zephyr **L.** Austin is the Social Media Marketing Manager for Alston-Hill Marketing Agency in Columbia, South Carolina. After graduating college with a Bachelor's in **English**, Zephyr worked as a freelance digital marketer for local restaurants before landing a position as a website copywriter at Alston-Hill. To further enhance and legitimize her self-taught digital media skills, Zephyr earned a **Master's** in Digital Marketing from Southern New Hampshire University. Although Zephyr loves the creative aspects of writing, web design and video production, she loves to help small business customers launch successful social media campaigns.

In 2016, Zephyr won **S**outh **C**arolina's **C**hamber of **C**ommerce's award for **B**est **D**igital **M**edia **P**rofessional. Her blog articles on social media marketing have been featured on *Forbes*, ***The Huffington Post***, and various other high-profile outlets. Her popular online classes and workshops are also well attended. Outside of work, Zephyr enjoys **Latin** dance classes, **volunteering** at a local animal shelter, and hosting dinner parties for friends and family.

Blog Article

Be the Most Interesting Person at Your Workplace

People make 1st impressions very quick, which means you have a short amount of time to get noticed. To be the most interesting person at your work place, you cannot just rely on being yourself. You might have to stretch yourself a bit. Use these tips to be the most fascinating person in the office or at your next company gathering:

1. **Look your best.** Dress average, and people will assume that you are average. We notice those who dress sharp. A perfect haircut catches our eye. Shine your shoes. Consider adding a new pair of our *Adair eyeglasses* to your look. Be bold in your clothing choices, but not radical. Have a unique, workplace appropriate style.

2. **Focus on others.** If you want people to think your fascinating, make them believe *their* fascinating. If you can make someone think they are the most interesting person in the room, you won't be soon forgotten, especially with our *Adair soft contact lenses*.

3. **Led an interesting life.** If your life is interesting, and you're willing to share it; you'll attract a variety of people. Travel, have unique experiences pursue interesting hobbies. There aren't two many people that do much beyond working and watching T-V. Not only will you be fascinating to others, but you'll also enjoy your life a lot more.

4. **Talk about things you're passsionate about.** Do you like teaching group fitness classes? Do you like to walk the beach or bike the trails while sportying our cool *Adair day-to-night sunglasses*? When you talk about things that interest you, your enthusiasm attacts people. What interests can you share with others? Share your enthusiasm with everyone and notice how well people respond to you.

Answers: Blog Article

Be the Most Interesting Person at Your Workplace

People make **first** impressions very **quickly**, which means you have a short amount of time to get noticed. To be the most interesting person at your **workplace**, you cannot just rely on being yourself. You might have to stretch yourself a bit. Use these tips to be the most fascinating person in the office or at your next company gathering:

1. **Look your best.** Dress average, and people will assume that you are average. We notice those who dress **sharply**. A perfect haircut catches our eye. Shine your shoes. Consider adding a new pair of our *Adair eyeglasses* to your look. Be bold in your clothing choices, but not radical. Have a unique, workplace appropriate style.

2. **Focus on others.** If you want people to think **you're** fascinating, make them believe *they're* fascinating. If you can make someone think they are the most interesting person in the room, you won't be soon forgotten, especially with our *Adair soft contact lenses*.

3. **Lead an interesting life.** If your life is interesting, and you're willing to share it, you'll attract a variety of people. Travel, have unique experiences **and** pursue interesting hobbies. There aren't **too** many people that do much beyond working and watching **TV**. Not only will you be fascinating to others, but you'll also enjoy your life a lot more.

4. **Talk about things you're passionate about.** Do you like teaching group fitness classes? Do you like to walk the beach or bike the trails while **sporting** our cool *Adair day-to-night sunglasses*? When you talk about things that interest you, your enthusiasm **attracts** people. What interests can you share with others? Share your enthusiasm with everyone and notice how well people respond to you.

Briefing Notes

Too: Marty Lutz, Operations Manager
From: Tia Long, program director
Date: February 21, 2020

Upcoming Meeeting with Debra Mitchell, General Manager

Purpose: Debra Mitchell has requested a meeting on Monday, February 24 at 2 p.m. in Conference Room 2221 with Marty Lutz and Tia Long to discuss listener complaints about inappropriate music and DJ banter during the *Hip Hop Wind Down*, 6-10 p.m. on Power 88 kjla.

Current Status: DJ Get Low and DJ Love have both been suspended with pay for the rest of the weak, until a resolution has been reached.

Essential Points:
- Listeners complained about the inappropriate and crude nature of the DJ banter between music breaks.
- The DJs played the entire explicit version of a wrap song instead of the clean version during the second hour of the show.
  - The DJs hanged up on callers who complained.
  - The receptionist counted forty (40) irate voice mail messages about their conduct.

Defensive Points:
- Program Director Tia Long talked to both DJs 1 month ago about their on-air antics.
- The DJs claim playing the explicit song was an acident. They was busy taking phone calls and didn't notice.

Recommmendations:
- Before the meeting, review the talent conduct policy with the DJs.
- Consider what further disciplinary action needs to be taken or if a brief suspension and second warning will sufice.

Answers: Briefing Notes

To: Marty Lutz, Operations Manager
From: Tia Long, **P**rogram **D**irector
Date: February 21, 2020

Upcoming <u>Meeting</u> with Debra Mitchell, General Manager

Purpose: Debra Mitchell has requested a meeting on Monday, February 24 at 2 p.m. in Conference Room 2221 with Marty Lutz and Tia Long to discuss listener complaints about inappropriate music and DJ banter during the *Hip Hop Wind Down*, 6-10 p.m. on Power 88 **<u>KJLA</u>**.

Current Status: DJ Get Low and DJ Love have both been suspended with pay for the rest of the **<u>week</u>**, until a resolution has been reached.

Essential Points:

- Listeners complained about the inappropriate and crude nature of the DJ banter between music breaks.
- The DJs played the entire explicit version of a **<u>rap</u>** song instead of the clean version during the second hour of the show.
- The DJs **<u>hung</u>** up on callers who complained. <-----**(<u>Change Bullets</u>)**
- The receptionist counted forty (40) irate voice mail messages about their conduct. <-----**(<u>Change Bullets</u>)**

Defensive Points:

- Program Director Tia Long talked to both DJs **<u>one</u>** month ago about their on-air antics.
- The DJs claim playing the explicit song was an **<u>accident</u>**. They **<u>were</u>** busy taking phone calls and didn't notice.

<u>Recommendations</u>:

- Before the meeting, review the talent conduct policy with the DJs.
- Consider what further disciplinary action needs to be taken or if a brief suspension and second warning will **<u>suffice</u>**.

Cover Letter

Erin Jackson
Cover Letter

Dear Hiring Manager,

I am applying for the human resources coordinator position for Stonewater Staffing and the opportunity it provides to design e-learning resources for employee training and development. In my current role, my primary duties include guiding employees through the benefits sign-up process and insuring that they follow through with reviewing and making changes to insurance benefits during the open enrollment period.

Recently, I developed five e-training classes that help employees change and access their benefit options. Prior to developing this online presentation; employees were required to attend face-to-face benefit meetings during the workday, prior to beginning work, or after hours. Based on what I know about your company, my ability to develop high-quality e-learning resources would be an asset.

After five years in my current position, I bring knowledge of many areas related to human resources, including interviewing, coordinating benefits, orienting new employees, and writing articles for the company newsletter.

I look forward to the oppertunity to meet you and to discuss how I can best serve your employees at Stonewater Staffing.

Sincerely,

Erin Jackson

Answers: Cover Letter

Erin Jackson
Cover Letter

Dear Hiring Manager,

I am applying for the **<u>Human Resources Coordinator</u>** position for Stonewater Staffing and the opportunity it provides to design e-learning resources for employee training and development. In my current role, my primary duties include guiding employees through the benefits sign-up process and **<u>ensuring</u>** that they follow through with reviewing and making changes to insurance benefits during the open enrollment period.

Recently, I developed five e-training classes that help employees change and access their benefit options. Prior to developing this online presentation, employees were required to attend face-to-face benefit meetings during the workday, prior to beginning work, or after hours. Based on what I know about your company, my ability to develop high-quality e-learning resources would be an asset.

After five years in my current position, I bring knowledge of many areas related to human resources, including interviewing, coordinating benefits, orienting new employees, and writing articles for the company newsletter.

I look forward to the **<u>opportunity</u>** to meet you and to discuss how I can best serve your employees at Stonewater Staffing.

Sincerely,

Erin Jackson

Résumé

Malik Robb
3931 Somewhere Street
Atlanta, GA 77993
(123) 456-7891
mrobb@email.com

SUMARY

Energetic Human Resources Generalist with more than five (5) years of experience recruiting accomplished employment candidates and maximizing departmental and organizational productivity.

EDUCASION

Coral Springs University, bachelor of arts in english, 1998-2002.

EXPERENCE

Watkins Media, HR Generalist
November 2010-present
- Select qualified candidates and conduct phone and in-person interviews, and perform reference checks for job candidates.
- Participate in exit interviews, gathering crucial information to improve department efficiencies and procedures.

CRANE & JENKINS, HR Specialist
May 2008-November 2010
- Reviewed, evaluated, and prioritized 50+ applications weekly.
- Posted job advertisements to major online job boards after analyzing job descriptions and requirements for acurate, relevant, and comprehensible information.

SKILS

- Microsoft Office Suite: Word, Outlook, Excel, and PowerPoint
- BambooHR
- Taleo and Workday
- Payroll Processing
- Recruitment and Retention

Answers: Résumé

Malik Robb
3931 Somewhere Street
Atlanta, GA 77993
(123) 456-7891
mrobb@email.com

SUMMARY

Energetic Human Resources Generalist with more than five (5) years of experience recruiting accomplished employment candidates and maximizing departmental and organizational productivity.

EDUCATION

Coral Springs University, **B**achelor of **A**rts **I**n **E**nglish, 1998-2002.

EXPERIENCE

Watkins Media, HR Generalist
November 2010-present

- Select qualified candidates and conduct phone and in-person interviews, and perform reference checks for job candidates.
- Participate in exit interviews, gathering crucial information to improve department efficiencies and procedures.

CRANE & JENKINS, HR Specialist
May 2008-November 2010

- Reviewed, evaluated, and prioritized 50+ applications weekly.
- Posted job advertisements to major online job boards after analyzing job descriptions and requirements for **accurate**, relevant, and comprehensible information.

SKILLS

- Microsoft Office Suite: Word, Outlook, Excel, and PowerPoint
- BambooHR
- Taleo and Workday
- Payroll Processing
- Recruitment and Retention

Email

To: Regional Managers

From: Alan Hansen, Vice President of Operations

Subject: Budget Meeting

We need a meeting to plan the operations budget for the coming year. It might take more than one meeting hammer out and finalize all budgets.

The first meeting will be in the dawson memorial conference room on the 2nd floor, March 11 at 10:00 a.m. Please clear your calendars for the rest of that afternoon to give us plenty of time to discuss each divisions proposed budget.

Please bring fifteen (15) printed copies of your budget projections and expenditures to the meeting. You should also be prepared to explain how your division can reduce operations expenses, or at the very least, maintain current productivity without spending moore money.

I look forward to seeing all of you on March 11th. If you have any questions before then, please contact my assistant Amanda greene at extension 1058.

Have a grate rest of your day!

Alan Hansen
Vice president of operations

Answers: Email

To: Regional Managers

From: Alan Hansen, Vice President of Operations

Subject: Budget Meeting

We need a meeting to plan the operations budget for the coming year. It might take more than one meeting **to** hammer out and finalize all budgets.

The first meeting will be in the **D**awson **M**emorial **C**onference **R**oom on the **second** floor, March 11 at **10 a.m.** Please clear your calendars for the rest of that afternoon to give us plenty of time to discuss each **division's** proposed budget.

Please bring fifteen (15) printed copies of your budget projections and expenditures to the meeting. You should also be prepared to explain how your division can reduce operations expenses, or at the very least, maintain current productivity without spending **more** money.

I look forward to seeing all of you on March **11.** If you have any questions before then, please contact my assistant Amanda **Greene** at extension 1058.

Have a **great** rest of your day!

Alan Hansen
Vice **President** of **Operations**

Business Letter

Rosita Gomez
Senior Project Manager
Lewis & Jenkins
555 Apple Lane
Seeattle, WV

May 31st, 2019

Mark Love
Senior Data Analyst
Cloud Motor Sales
100 Orange Circle
Seattle, WA

Dear Mr. Love…

It is my pleasure to strongly recommmend Charity Jones for the Junior Data Analyst role with Cloud Motor Sales. I am Rosita Gomez, a senior project manager at Crane & Jenkins. After twelve (13) years of experience in the tech industry, I have seen many young professionals come and go. Ms. Jones is 1 individual I have worked with who uniquely stands out.

During our time together, Chloe displayed great talents in data analytics. When we first met, I was immediately impressed with Charity and her understanding of data analysis to acheive results for our company.

I am absolutely confident that Charity would be a great fit at Clown Motor Sales. Not only will she bring the kind of skills and experiences your looking for in an applicant, she will quickly become an assett and help your company grow in any way she can. If you need more information or specific examples, please do not hesitate to contact me at 555-111-9999.

Sincerely,

Rosita Gomez
Senior Project Manager

Answers: Business Letter

Rosita Gomez
Senior Project Manager
Lewis & Jenkins
555 Apple Lane
Seattle, **WA**

May **31,** 2019

Mark Love
Senior Data Analyst
Cloud Motor Sales
100 Orange Circle
Seattle, WA

Dear Mr. Love**,**

It is my pleasure to strongly **recommend** Charity Jones for the Junior Data Analyst role with Cloud Motor Sales. I am Rosita Gomez, a senior project manager at Crane & Jenkins. After twelve **(12)** years of experience in the tech industry, I have seen many young professionals come and go. Ms. Jones is **one** individual I have worked with who uniquely stands out.

During our time together, **Charity** displayed great talents in data analytics. When we first met, I was immediately impressed with Charity and her understanding of data analysis to **achieve** results for our company.

I am absolutely confident that Charity would be a great fit at **Cloud** Motor Sales. Not only will she bring the kind of skills and experiences **you're** looking for in an applicant, she will quickly become an **asset** and help your company grow in any way she can. If you need more information or specific examples, please do not hesitate to contact me at 555-111-9999.

Sincerely,

Rosita Gomez
Senior Project Manager

Sales Letter

Merrito's Pizza Parlor
3515 W. 5th Street
Texarkana, AR 34221
(214)749-9987

Treat Your Team to a Pizza Party!

Dear Pizza Lovers:

To show appreciation to all of your employees, why not give them a pizza party? Everybody loves pizza, and nobody beats our delicious slices and affordable prices!

From now until the end of the year, businesses in *Pleasant Towne Office Centre* can take advantage of our group sales offer that feeds 15-20 people. When you order, just use the code GMP20.

Here's What You Get in the *Pleasant Towne Office Centre Group Special* for only $25:
*   One extra-large 1-topping pizza
*   One extra-large signature pizza
*   24 breadsticks and sauces

Need to feed more people? To this base group order, you can add additional medium pizzas for only $5 each from our 1-topping and signature pizza selections. We also offer vegan and gluten-free options at additional costs. Since the *Centre* is only five blocks away, delivery is free.

Don't delay! Please consider **Merrito's Pizza Parlor** for your next pizza purchase. You can call or come buy to place your group order. This offer is not available for online ordering, and is limited to businesses and employees within the *Pleasant Towne Office Centre*.

Call us today at (214)749-9987.
We look forward to serving you!

Answers: Sales Letter

Merrito's Pizza Parlor
3515 W. 5th Street
Texarkana, AR 34221
(214)749-9987

Treat Your Team to a Pizza Party!

Dear Pizza Lovers:

To show appreciation to all of your employees, why not give them a pizza party? Everybody loves pizza, and nobody beats our delicious slices and affordable prices!

From now until the end of the year, businesses in *Pleasant Towne Office Centre* can take advantage of our group sales offer that feeds 15-20 people. When you order, just use the code GMP20.

Here's What You Get in the *Pleasant Towne Office Centre Group Special* for only $25:
- One extra-large 1-topping pizza
- One extra-large signature pizza
- 24 breadsticks and sauces

Need to feed more people? To this base group order, you can add additional medium pizzas for only $5 each from our 1-topping and signature pizza selections. We also offer vegan and gluten-free options at additional costs. Since the *Centre* is only five blocks away, delivery is free.

Don't delay! Please consider **Merrito's Pizza Parlor** for your next pizza purchase. You can call or come **by** to place your group order. This offer is not available for online ordering, and is limited to businesses and employees within the *Pleasant Towne Office Centre.*

Call us today at (214)749-9987.
We look forward to serving you!

Press Release

For Immediate Release

Rapper Big 2-Much Takes Over Urban Radio

ATLANTA, GA; *March 8, 2020*—Radio Superstar Broadcast Network named popular social media rapper, Big Too-Much as Director of Urban Radio Programming. Donell Richardson, (*aka Big 2-Much*) will report to Gloria Nayles, Chief Programmming Executive.

In this role, Donell will oversea urban radio programming, including hip hop and R & B for seventy-five (75) radio stations in major metropolitan markets across the country. He will start working on April 10th, 2020.

"We're excited to welcome Donell to our team. His background in broadcast media, paired with his knowledge of social media production and marketing, will be invaluable as we continue to provide programming that reflects our diverse audience and the local communities we serve, said Nayles.

Before gaining a huge social media following, Donell graduated from Niles College with a bachelors in communications, and worked for HOT POWER 93.1 fm Nashville for five (5) years as a weekend radio talent and Urban Promotions Director.

About RSBN
Radio Superior Broadcast Network offers three hundred fifty mid-sized radio stations, urban terrestrial radio, and digital content. Each month, RBSN reaches over one hundred twenty million people through traditional radio and online streaming. Having initially launched in 1978; RSBN is the only remaining minority owned radio broadcasting company in the country.

Media Contact: Fernando Grace
Phone: 212-223-0000
Emale: fgrace@rsbn.com

Answers: Press Release

For Immediate Release

Rapper Big 2-Much Takes Over Urban Radio

ATLANTA, GA; *March 8, 2020*—Radio Superstar Broadcast Network named popular social media rapper, **Big 2**-Much as Director of Urban Radio Programming. Donell Richardson, (*aka Big 2-Much*) will report to Gloria Nayles, Chief **Programming** Executive.

In this role, Donell will **oversee** urban radio programming, including hip hop and R & B for seventy-five (75) radio stations in major metropolitan markets across the country. He will start working on April **10**, 2020.

"We're excited to welcome Donell to our team. His background in broadcast media, paired with his knowledge of social media production and marketing, will be invaluable as we continue to provide programming that reflects our diverse audience and the local communities we serve**,"** said Nayles.

Before gaining a huge social media following, Donell graduated from Niles College with a **Bachelor's** in **Communications**, and worked for HOT POWER 93.1 **FM** Nashville for five (5) years as a weekend radio talent and Urban Promotions Director.

About RSBN
Radio **Superstar** Broadcast Network offers **350** mid-sized radio stations, urban terrestrial radio, and digital content. Each month, **RSBN** reaches over **120** million people through traditional radio and online streaming. Having initially launched in 1978**,** RSBN is the only remaining minority owned radio broadcasting company in the country.

Media Contact: Fernando Grace
Phone: 212-223-0000
Email: fgrace@rsbn.com

Grammar Assessments

Circle the answer or fill in the blank.

Read the directions for each section,

if applicable.

Start Proofreading Now!

www.arhampton.com/books

Grammar Assessment I

1. Most _____ in the Northeast have public transportation systems.
   a. citys
   b. cities
   c. city

2. Steve had to buy Christmas gifts for several of his _____.
   a. brothers-in-law
   b. brother-in-law
   c. brother-in-laws

3. Jonathan and _____ thought that skydiving might be fun to try.
   a. I
   b. me
   c. her

4. Everyone must bring _____ own chair to the outdoor jazz concert.
   a. their
   b. our
   c. his or her

5. The company launched _____ new environmental campaign today.
   a. its
   b. their
   c. it's

6. When LeBron dunked the ball into the net, the fans _____ wild.
   a. go
   b. went

7. By the time Chad is finished cramming for finals, he _____ for seven hours.
   a. studied
   b. will have studied

8. As he dashed through the parking lot toward the building, Charles hoped that the meeting had not already_____.
    a. begun
    b. begin
    c. began

9. The coins in the jar on top of the microwave_____to be counted and rolled.
    a. needs
    b. need
    c. needed

10. One of those sandwiches in the refrigerator_____for you.
    a. is
    b. are
    c. not

11. Choose the sentence in which all the **commas** are used correctly.
    a. The 1985 Ford which has ignition trouble is hard to start.
    b. The 1985 Ford, which has ignition trouble is hard to start.
    c. The 1985 Ford, which has ignition trouble, is hard to start.

12. Choose the sentence in which all the **commas** are used correctly.
    a. Robert, my buddy from college, is now the registrar.
    b. Applicants, who arrive after four o'clock will have to return tomorrow.
    c. We synchronized our watches, and left.

13. Choose the sentence in which all the **commas** are used correctly.
    a. Your plan for a day-care center by the way, is the best I have ever seen.
    b. Your plan for a day-care center, by the way is the best I have ever seen.
    c. Your plan for a day-care center, by the way, is the best I have ever seen.

Directions: In #14-16, cross out and correct all of the misspelled words.

14. The morning star seemed to loose some of it's brilliance.

15. Marci has trouble excepting complements; she blushes and becomes quite.

16. Is you're brother taking the teaching position he was offered?

17. **Occupation** is another word for_____.
> a. home
> b. job
> c. associate

18. Something that is **benign** is_____.
> a. cancerous
> b. dangerous
> c. non-threatening

19. There is a huge **<u>chasm</u>** between the rich and the poor.
> a. gap
> b. demean
> c. bridge

20. Please **<u>expel</u>** that noisy group.
> a. refer
> b. arrest
> c. oust

Directions: Correct all **capitalization**, **grammar**, **punctuation** and **spelling** errors in the sentences below. Write **"C"** in the space provided if there are no errors.

21. Helen past the GED exem, and became a grate call center supervisor.

22. Duncan Haynes was late for work today, which was unusual.

23. Ms. greene are going to the supply closet to get some paper.

24. jerome is a vegetarian, but he love Chilli Cheese fries.

25. Although she pretends to like it Adrianne dont like going to company lunch's Potlucks or holiday parties.

Answers: Grammar I

1. Most _____ in the Northeast have public transportation systems.
    a. citys
    b. <u>cities</u>
    c. city

2. Steve had to buy Christmas gifts for several of his _____.
    a. <u>brothers-in-law</u>
    b. brother-in-law
    c. brother-in-laws

3. Jonathan and _____ thought that skydiving might be fun to try.
    a. <u>I</u>
    b. me
    c. her

4. Everyone must bring _____ own chair to the outdoor jazz concert.
    a. their
    b. our
    c. <u>his or her</u>

5. The company launched _____ new environmental campaign today.
    a. <u>its</u>
    b. their
    c. it's

6. When LeBron dunked the ball into the net, the fans _____ wild.
    a. go
    b. <u>went</u>

7. By the time Chad is finished cramming for finals, he _____ for seven hours.
    a. studied
    b. <u>will have studied</u>

8. As he dashed through the parking lot toward the building, Charles hoped that the meeting had not already_____.
    a. <u>begun</u>
    b. begin
    c. began

9. The coins in the jar on top of the microwave_____to be counted and rolled.
    a. needs
    b. <u>need</u>
    c. needed

10. One of those sandwiches in the refrigerator_____for you.
    a. <u>is</u>
    b. are
    c. not

11. Choose the sentence in which all the **commas** are used correctly.
    a. The 1985 Ford which has ignition trouble is hard to start.
    b. The 1985 Ford, which has ignition trouble is hard to start.
    c. <u>The 1985 Ford, which has ignition trouble, is hard to start.</u>

12. Choose the sentence in which all the **commas** are used correctly.
    a. <u>Robert, my buddy from college, is now the registrar.</u>
    b. Applicants, who arrive after four o'clock will have to return tomorrow.
    c. We synchronized our watches, and left.

13. Choose the sentence in which all the **commas** are used correctly.
    a. Your plan for a day-care center by the way, is the best I have ever seen.
    b. Your plan for a day-care center, by the way is the best I have ever seen.
    c. <u>Your plan for a day-care center, by the way, is the best I have ever seen.</u>

Directions: In #14-16, cross out and correct all of the misspelled words.

14. The morning star seemed to ~~loose~~ **(lose)** some of ~~it's~~ **(its)** brilliance.

15. Marci has trouble ~~excepting~~ **(accepting)** ~~complements~~; **(compliments)** she blushes and becomes ~~quite~~ **(quiet)**.

16. Is ~~you're~~ **(your)** brother taking the teaching position he was offered?

17. **Occupation** is another word for_____.
    a. home
    b. job
    c. associate

18. Something that is **benign** is_____.
    a. cancerous
    b. dangerous
    c. non-threatening

19. There is a huge **chasm** between the rich and the poor.
    a. gap
    b. demean
    c. bridge

20. Please **expel** that noisy group.
    a. refer
    b. arrest
    c. oust

Directions: Correct all **capitalization**, **grammar**, **punctuation** and **spelling** errors in the sentences below. Write **"C"** in the space provided if there are no errors.

---

21. Helen ~~past~~ **(passed)** the GED ~~exem~~ **(exam),** and became a ~~grate~~ **(great)** call center supervisor.

22. Duncan Haynes was late for work today, which was unusual. **(C) Correct**

23. Ms. ~~greene~~ **(Greene)** ~~are~~ **(is)** going to the supply closet to get some paper.

24. ~~jerome~~ **(Jerome)** is a vegetarian, but he ~~love~~ **(loves)** ~~Chilli~~ **(chilli)** Cheese **(cheese)** fries.

25. Although she pretends to like it**(,)** Adrianne ~~dont~~ **(doesn't)** like going to company ~~lunch's~~ **(lunches)**, ~~Potlucks~~ **(potlucks)** or holiday parties.

Grammar Assessment II

1. Choose the sentence in which all the **apostrophes** are used correctly.
   - a. I'm spending this week's paycheck on rent.
   - b. Im spending this weeks' paycheck on rent.
   - c. I'm spending this weeks paycheck on rent.

2. Choose the sentence in which all the **apostrophes** are used correctly.
   - a. Todd's and Diane's house has two bedrooms.
   - b. Todd and Diane's house has two bedroom's.
   - c. Todd and Diane's house has two bedrooms.

3. Which group of words is **spelled** correctly?
   - a. amateur, villain, seiz
   - b. argument, paradize, committee
   - c. writing, aggravate, pursue

4. There is conflict_____operations and marketing.
   - a. among
   - b. between

5. Tim laughed when he saw the way that_____had dressed for the Halloween party.
   - a. Serena and I
   - b. Serena and me

6. When Jamal came looking for_____, we had already left.
   - a. Karen and me
   - b. Karen and I

7. Choose the sentence that **includes an error**.
   - a. My sisters and brothers-in-law met me at the airport.
   - b. She is rich, beautiful and has talent.
   - c. Neither the cats nor the dog has eaten breakfast.

8. Choose the **correct** sentence.

 a. I am not guilty, your honor.

 b. I am not guilty, Your Honor.

 c. I am not guilty, your Honor.

9. John smokes cigars even though he knows_____.

 a. they are bad for you.

 b. smoking is bad for him.

 c. it is bad for him.

10. Choose the sentence in which all the **commas are used correctly**.

 a. Bring green beans rolls, and salad to Sashas' for dinner at eight.

 b. Bring green, beans, rolls and salad to Sasha's for dinner at eight.

 c. Bring green beans, rolls, and salad to Sasha's for dinner at eight.

11. Choose the **correct** sentence.

 a. Patiently waiting in line, hoping to buy tickets for the musical.

 b. They patiently waiting in line, hoping to buy tickets for the musical.

 c. They patiently waited in line, hoping to buy tickets for the musical.

12. Dave and_____will make our presentation this afternoon.

 a. myself

 b. I

 c. me

13. _____did you verify the agenda with before the meeting?

 a. Whom

 b. Who

 c. Whomever

14. Choose the sentence that **includes an error**.

 a. We players want to buy a gift for our coach.

 b. She has forgotten to turn off the lights again.

 c. Your not going to believe this story.

15. When it comes to highway tolls, I differ_____Senator Freiling.

    a. on
    b. with
    c. from

16. The candidate's record on health-care reform is what_____Margaret.
    a. impress
    b. impresses

17. One of the dentists_____close to her office.
    a. live
    b. lives

18. When writing a research paper, you must first_____your sources.
    a. cite
    b. sight
    c. site

19. Ask the accountants to_____their materials in the next office.
    a. set
    b. sit

20. Each operator worked on_____pallet.
    a. his
    b. a
    c. their

21. Choose the **correct spelling** of each word.
    a. potatos / potatoes
    b. perceive / percieve
    c. seperate / separate

22. **Choose the sentence in which all the commas are used correctly.**
    a. Your plan for a day-care center by the way, is the best I have ever seen.
    b. Your plan for a day-care center, by the way is the best I have ever seen.
    c. Your plan for a day-care center, by the way, is the best I have ever seen.

23. Choose the sentence in which all the **commas are used correctly.**

    a. Because I did not know that Jackie, my roommate from college, was coming to visit me I went to Columbia South Carolina for the weekend.

    b. Because I did not know that Jackie, my roommate from college, was coming to visit me, I went to Columbia, South Carolina for the weekend.

    c. Because I did not know that Jackie my roommate from college was coming to visit me, I went to Columbia, South Carolina for the weekend.

24. **Directions:** Fill the blank with the **correct word** for each sentence below.

appeal	variety	procedure	sufficient
establish	wholesome	renew	assume
potential	possess	resources	justify

a. Without speaking to the teacher, you cannot_____the student is telling the truth.

b. *Brown Sugar Bake Shop* sells a_____of cupcakes, cookies, and pie slices.

c. Mark needs to_____good credit to purchase his dream car.

d. To restore your borrowing privileges, you must_____your library card.

25. **Directions:** Correct all **spelling, capitalization,** and **punctuation** errors below.

Hear is the information about the support group meeting on saturday, June 2, 2019. Please attend to discuss very important issues. They're will also be lots of opportunites to network. We will talk laugh and support each other. The meeting will be held at the Western conference center. Parking is to the right of the Building. From our office, travel North to Brook street Go threw 2 stoplights, and turn right on Main Street. The conference center is on you're left. Several brakes are scheduled throughout the day. Its a good idea to bring cash for lunch, since only breakfast will be provided for free from our sponsors.

Answers: Grammar II

1. Choose the sentence in which all the **apostrophes** are used correctly.
   a. I'm spending this week's paycheck on rent.
   b. Im spending this weeks' paycheck on rent.
   c. I'm spending this weeks paycheck on rent.

2. Choose the sentence in which all the **apostrophes** are used correctly.
   a. Todd's and Diane's house has two bedrooms.
   b. Todd and Diane's house has two bedroom's.
   c. Todd and Diane's house has two bedrooms.

3. Which group of words is **spelled** correctly?
   a. amateur, villain, seiz
   b. argument, paradize, committee
   c. writing, aggravate, pursue

4. There is conflict_____operations and marketing.
   a. among
   b. between

5. Tim laughed when he saw the way that_____had dressed for the Halloween party.
   a. Serena and I
   b. Serena and me

6. When Jamal came looking for_____, we had already left.
   a. Karen and me
   b. Karen and I

7. Choose the sentence that **includes an error**.
   a. My sisters and brothers-in-law met me at the airport.
   b. She is rich, beautiful and has talent.
   c. Neither the cats nor the dog has eaten breakfast.

8. Choose the **correct** sentence.
    a. I am not guilty, your honor.
    b. <u>I am not guilty, Your Honor.</u>
    c. I am not guilty, your Honor.

9. John smokes cigars even though he knows_____ .
    a. they are bad for you.
    b. <u>smoking is bad for him.</u>
    c. it is bad for him.

10. Choose the sentence in which all the **commas are used correctly**.
    a. Bring green beans rolls, and salad to Sashas' for dinner at eight.
    b. Bring green, beans, rolls and salad to Sasha's for dinner at eight.
    c. <u>Bring green beans, rolls, and salad to Sasha's for dinner at eight.</u>

11. Choose the **correct** sentence.
    a. Patiently waiting in line, hoping to buy tickets for the musical.
    b. They patiently waiting in line, hoping to buy tickets for the musical.
    c. <u>They patiently waited in line, hoping to buy tickets for the musical.</u>

12. Dave and_____will make our presentation this afternoon.
    a. myself
    b. <u>I</u>
    c. me

13. _____did you verify the agenda with before the meeting?
    a. <u>Whom</u>
    b. Who
    c. Whomever

14. Choose the sentence that includes an error.
    a. We players want to buy a gift for our coach.
    b. She has forgotten to turn off the lights again.
    c. <u>Your not going to believe this story.</u>

15. When it comes to highway tolls, I differ_____Senator Freiling.
    a. on
    b. with
    c. <u>from</u>

16. The candidate's record on health-care reform is what_____Margaret.
    a. impress
    b. <u>impresses</u>

17. One of the dentists_____close to her office.
    a. live
    b. <u>lives</u>

18. When writing a research paper, you must first_____your sources.
    a. <u>cite</u>
    b. sight
    c. site

19. Ask the accountants to_____their materials in the next office.
    a. <u>set</u>
    b. sit

20. Each operator worked on_____pallet.
    a. his
    b. <u>a</u>
    c. their

21. Choose the correct spelling of each word.
    a. potatos / **<u>potatoes</u>**
    b. **<u>perceive</u>** / percieve
    c. seperate / **<u>separate</u>**

22. Choose the sentence in which all the **commas are used correctly**.
    a. Your plan for a day-care center by the way, is the best I have ever seen.
    b. Your plan for a day-care center, by the way is the best I have ever seen.
    c. <u>Your plan for a day-care center, by the way, is the best I have ever seen.</u>

23. Choose the sentence in which all the **commas are used correctly**.

    a. Because I did not know that Jackie, my roommate from college, was coming to visit me I went to Columbia South Carolina for the weekend.

    b. **<u>Because I did not know that Jackie, my roommate from college, was coming to visit me, I went to Columbia, South Carolina for the weekend.</u>**

    c. Because I did not know that Jackie my roommate from college was coming to visit me, I went to Columbia, South Carolina for the weekend.

24. **Directions:** Fill the blank with the **correct word** for each sentence below.

    a. Without speaking to the teacher, you cannot **<u>assume</u>** the student is telling the truth.

    b. *Brown Sugar Bake Shop* sells a **<u>variety</u>** of cupcakes, cookies, and pie slices.

    c. Mark needs to **<u>establish</u>** good credit to purchase his dream car.

    d. To restore your borrowing privileges, you must **<u>renew</u>** your library card.

25. **Directions:** Correct all **spelling**, **capitalization**, and **punctuation** errors below.

~~Hear~~ **(Here)** is the information about the support group meeting on ~~Saturday~~ **(Saturday),** June 2, 2019. Please attend to discuss very important issues. ~~They're~~ **(There)** will also be lots of ~~opportunites~~ **(opportunities)** to network. We will **talk(,) laugh(,) and** support each other. The meeting will be held at the Western **(Conference) (Center)** ~~conference center~~. Parking is to the right of the ~~Building~~ **(building).** From our office, travel ~~North~~ **(north)** to Brook ~~street~~ **(Street).** Go ~~threw~~ **(through)** ~~2~~ **(two)** stoplights, and turn right on Main Street. The conference center is on ~~you're~~ **(your)** left. Several ~~brakes~~ **(breaks)** are scheduled throughout the day. ~~Its~~ **(It's)** a good idea to bring cash for lunch, since only breakfast will be provided for free from our sponsors.

Grammar Assessment III

Directions: Choose a word that is similar to the **bold highlighted** word in the sentence.

1. She's such a **novice**. She's new to this.
    a. beginner
    b. average
    c. oust

2. That was such a **mediocre** performance.
    a. great
    b. average
    c. terrible

3. Thanks for your **consideration**.
    a. negative review
    b. positive words
    c. careful thought

4. Mark decided to **extricate** himself from the argument.
    a. engage
    b. remove
    c. mediate

5. Dana **reiterated** the boss's directions.
    a. disliked
    b. avoided
    c. repeated

6. Whenever my family_____to a baseball game, we all_____hot dogs and pretzels.
    a. go, gets
    b. goes, get

7. Each of those desserts_____low in calories and fat.
    a. are
    b. is

8. Neither the buyer nor the seller_____with the lawyer's suggestion for the closing date on the house.
    a. agree
    b. agrees

9. Ray, along with two of his friends, _____to visit Miami.
    a. plans
    b. plan

10. The leaves of the cherry tree_____poisonous.
    a. is
    b. are

Directions: Circle or underline the **appropriate** word.

11. We are **(anxious, eager)** to participate in the sales training program.

12. The reorganization will **(affect, effect)** the home office as well as the regional offices.

13. Do you **(imply, infer)** by your complaints that you don't want to use the new computer software program?

14. I suggest that you **(accept, except)** the job offer from the West Coast.

15. The committee decided it will need more **(capital, capitol)** to finance the new product line.

16. Service, not price, is the main **(criteria, criterion)** we use when we make our purchasing decisions.

Directions: Correct all **misspelled words** in the following sentences.

17. Weather or not it rains, were going to the performance at the outdoor theater.

18. They are suppose to set in the last row because there late.

19. Joel hoped that his knew job on Sundays would not effect his grade-point average.

20. David new he loved Kay win she helped a cat out of the drain.

21. Is you're sister weighting to get married before graduating?

Directions: Choose the sentence in which **capital letters** and **punctuation** have been used **correctly**.

22.
   a. Arthur Ashe was the first African-American man to win three Grand Slam titles, the U.S. Open in 1968; the Australian Open in 1970; and Wimbledon in 1975.
   b. Arthur Ashe was the first African American man to win three Grand Slam titles: the U.S. Open in 1968, the Australian Open in 1970, and Wimbledon in 1975.
   c. Arthur Ashe was the first African-american man to win three Grand Slam Titles: the u.s. open in 1968, the australian open in 1970, and wimbledon in 1975.

23.
   a. Last Fall, I withdrew from chemistry II.
   b. Last fall, I withdrew from Chemistry II.
   c. Last Fall I withdrew from chemistry II.

24.
   a. The Tuft's university lecture series coordinator invited Howard Zinn, author of A people's history of the united states, to speak at Ballou hall on May 6.
   b. The Tufts university lecture series coordinator invited Howard Zinn, author of "A people's history of the united states," to speak at Ballou hall on May 6.
   c. The Tufts University Lecture Series coordinator invited Howard Zinn, author of "A People's History of the United States," to speak at Ballou Hall on May 6.

Directions: Choose the sentence in which all of the **verbs** are **correct**.

25.

    a. Advisors will tell their students to register early so that they got the classes they wanted.

    b. Advisors will tell their students to register early so that they can get the classes they want.

26.

    a. In 1835, Charles Darwin explored the Galapagos Islands, and in 1850 he writes *Origin of Species*.

    b. In 1835, Charles Darwin explored the Galapagos Islands, and in 1850 he wrote *Origin of Species*.

27.

    a. The virus mutated so rapidly that it developed a resistance to most vaccines.

    b. The virus mutated so rapidly that it develops a resistance to most vaccines.

28.

    a. In the interview, the star of the film explained the stunt work and talked about the special effects. However, she never mentions her costars.

    b. In the interview, the star of the film explained the stunt work and talked about the special effects. However, she never mentioned her costars.

29.

    a. Tonight, Yvette had hoped to read *The Song of Solomon* before going to bed.

    b. Tonight, Yvette hopes to read *The Song of Solomon* before going to bed.

Directions: Choose the sentence in which all the **punctuation** is correct.

30.

    a. If you dont dot your i's; they will look like 1's.

    b. If you don't dot your i's, they will look like 1's.

    c. If you don't dot your is they will look like Is.

31.

    a. True friends exhibit four main qualities; openness, trust, loyalty, and love.

    b. True friends exhibit four main qualities: openness, trust, loyalty; and love.

    c. True friends exhibit four main qualities: openness, trust, loyalty, and love.

32.
    a. Brandon was ready to go to his job interview, but there was one small problem,
       he couldn't find his car keys.
    b. Brandon was ready to go to his job interview, but there was one small problem;
       he couldn't find his car keys.
    c. Brandon was ready to go to his job interview but there was one small problem:
       he couldnt find his car keys.

33.
    a. "Where is the nearest gas station?" Tanya asked.
    b. 'Where is the nearest gas station?" Tanya asked.
    c. "Where is the nearest gas station? Tanya asked."

34.
    a. The bridal bouquets included her favorite flowers; roses, carnations and tulips.
    b. The bridal bouquets included her favorite flowers: roses, carnations and tulips.
    c. The bridal bouquets included her favorite flowers...roses, carnations and tulips.

Directions: Insert the **correct punctuation** throughout the following paragraph.

35. Punctuation marks have often been compared to road signs they direct the reader
through the document Imagine if you were driving through your citys streets and
there were no traffic signs chaos would result Its important to use the appropriate
signs and then your reader will quickly and efficiently be able to read and
comprehend your document Don't you find it rather difficult reading this exercise
with no punctuation marks

36. I want a doctor who doesn't double book_____ patients.
    a. his or her
    b. his

37. What qualifications does one need to be a_____?
    a. fireman
    b. fire fighter

38. Alaina loves to write and dreams of becoming a famous_____.
    a. poet
    b. female poet

39. Please address this invitation to_____.
   a. Mr. and Mrs. G. Brown
   b. Eleanor and Mr. Brown
   c. Mr. and Mrs. Brown

40. Four_____ and six men sat on the discussion panel.
   a. women
   b. ladies
   c. girls

Directions: Choose the correctly written sentence.

41.
   a. 42 people signed up for the fitness workshop.
   b. Forty-two people signed up for the fitness workshop.

42.
   a. The three catering trucks will arrive at 12 noon.
   b. The 3 catering trucks will arrive at 12 p.m.

43.
   a. Tomorrow, 150 high school seniors, five mentors and 13 coaches will arrive.
   b. Tomorrow, 150 high school seniors, 5 mentors and 13 coaches will arrive.

44.
   a. One communications textbook costs $225.00.
   b. One communications textbook costs $225.

Directions: Make all necessary **changes** to expressions of **numbers**.

45. Yesterday my administrative assistant contacted the Joe C. Thompson Conference Center at 4455 3rd Street in Austin to determine whether it had suitable space available for July 10th-13th. She indicated that they had a meeting room one hundred fifty feet by fifty feet that is available. There is also no restriction on time limit for use of the room if we conclude the hearings by 7:00 p.m. each day.

Directions: Correct the **capitalization**, **punctuation** (e.g. commas, apostrophes, quotation marks) and **spelling errors** in the sentences below.

46. Please scend copies of the report before next thursday.

47. Alexander pope wrote to err is human, to forgive divine.

48. Martha's manager a grate guy is retiring next year.

49. You should head North when you reach the Town Hall.

50. immediately the fire department was called to the scene.

Answers: Grammar III

Directions: Choose a word that is similar to the bold highlighted word in the sentence.

1. She's such a **novice**. She's new to this.
    a. beginner
    b. average
    c. oust

2. That was such a **mediocre** performance.
    a. great
    b. average
    c. terrible

3. Thanks for your **consideration**.
    a. negative review
    b. positive words
    c. careful thought

4. Mark decided to **extricate** himself from the argument.
    a. engage
    b. remove
    c. mediate

5. Dana **reiterated** the boss's directions.
    a. disliked
    b. avoided
    c. repeated

6. Whenever my family_____to a baseball game, we all_____hot dogs and pretzels.
    a. go, gets
    b. goes, get

7. Each of those desserts_____ low in calories and fat.
      a. are
      b. <u>is</u>

8. Neither the buyer nor the seller_____ with the lawyer's suggestion for the closing date on the house.
      a. agree
      b. <u>agrees</u>

9. Ray, along with two of his friends_____, to visit Miami.
      a. <u>plans</u>
      b. plan

10. The leaves of the cherry tree_____ poisonous.
      a. is
      b. <u>are</u>

Directions: Circle or underline the **appropriate** word.

11. We are **(anxious, <u>eager</u>)** to participate in the sales training program.

12. The reorganization will **(<u>affect</u>, effect)** the home office as well as the regional offices.

13. Do you **(<u>imply</u>, infer)** by your complaints that you don't want to use the new computer software program?

14. I suggest that you **(<u>accept</u>, except)** the job offer from the West Coast.

15. The committee decided it will need more **(<u>capital</u>, capitol)** to finance the new product line.

16. Service, not price, is the main **(criteria, <u>criterion</u>)** we use when we make our purchasing decisions.

Directions: Correct all **misspelled words** in the following sentences.

17. ~~Weather~~ **(Whether)** or not it rains, ~~were~~ **(we are)** going to the performance at the outdoor theater.

18. They are ~~suppose~~ **(supposed)** to ~~set~~ **(sit)** in the last row because ~~there~~ **(they're)** late.

19. Joel hoped that his ~~knew~~ **(new)** job on Sundays would not ~~effect~~ **(affect)** his gradepoint average.

20. David ~~new~~ **(knew)** he loved Kay ~~win~~ **(when)** she helped a cat out of the drain.

21. Is ~~you're~~ **(your)** sister ~~weighting~~ **(waiting)** to get married before graduating?

Directions: Choose the sentence in which **capital letters** and **punctuation** have been used **correctly**.

22.
   a. Arthur Ashe was the first African-American man to win three Grand Slam titles, the U.S. Open in 1968; the Australian Open in 1970; and Wimbledon in 1975.
   b. **Arthur Ashe was the first African American man to win three Grand Slam titles: the U.S. Open in 1968, the Australian Open in 1970, and Wimbledon in 1975.**
   c. Arthur Ashe was the first African-american man to win three Grand Slam Titles: the u.s. open in 1968, the australian open in 1970, and wimbledon in 1975.

23.
   a. Last Fall, I withdrew from chemistry II.
   b. **Last fall, I withdrew from Chemistry II.**
   c. Last Fall I withdrew from chemistry II.

24.
   a. The Tuft's university lecture series coordinator invited Howard Zinn, author of A people's history of the united states, to speak at Ballou hall on May 6.
   b. The Tufts university lecture series coordinator invited Howard Zinn, author of "A people's history of the united states," to speak at Ballou hall on May 6.
   c. The Tufts University Lecture Series coordinator invited Howard Zinn, author of "A People's History of the United States," to speak at Ballou Hall on May 6.

....
Directions: Choose the sentence in which all of the **verbs** are **correct**.
....

25.
   a. Advisors will tell their students to register early so that they got the classes they wanted.
   b. Advisors will tell their students to register early so that they can get the classes they want.

26.
   a. In 1835, Charles Darwin explored the Galapagos Islands, and in 1850, he writes *Origin of Species*.
   b. In 1835, Charles Darwin explored the Galapagos Islands, and in 1850, he wrote *Origin of Species*.

27.
   a. The virus mutated so rapidly that it developed a resistance to most vaccines.
   b. The virus mutated so rapidly that it develops a resistance to most vaccines.

28.
   a. In the interview, the star of the film explained the stunt work and talked about the special effects. However, she never mentions her costars.
   b. In the interview, the star of the film explained the stunt work and talked about the special effects. However, she never mentioned her costars.

29.
   a. Tonight, Yvette had hoped to read *The Song of Solomon* before going to bed.
   b. Tonight, Yvette hopes to read *The Song of Solomon* before going to bed.

Directions: Choose the sentence in which all the **punctuation** is correct.

30.

    a. If you dont dot your i's; they will look like 1's.

    b. If you don't dot your i's, they will look like 1's.

    c. If you don't dot your is they will look like ls.

31.

    a. True friends exhibit four main qualities; openness, trust, loyalty, and love.

    b. True friends exhibit four main qualities: openness, trust, loyalty; and love.

    c. True friends exhibit four main qualities: openness, trust, loyalty, and love.

32.

    a. Brandon was ready to go to his job interview, but there was one small problem, he couldn't find his car keys.

    b. Brandon was ready to go to his job interview, but there was one small problem; he couldn't find his car keys.

    c. Brandon was ready to go to his job interview but there was one small problem: he couldnt find his car keys.

33.

    a. "Where is the nearest gas station?" Tanya asked.

    b. 'Where is the nearest gas station?" Tanya asked.

    c. "Where is the nearest gas station? Tanya asked."

34.

    a. The bridal bouquets included her favorite flowers; roses, carnations, and tulips.

    b. The bridal bouquets included her favorite flowers: roses, carnations, and tulips.

    c. The bridal bouquets included her favorite flowers...roses, carnations, and tulips.

Directions: Insert the **correct punctuation** throughout the following paragraph.

35. Punctuation marks have often been compared to road signs; they direct the reader through the document. Imagine if you were driving through your **city's** streets and there were no traffic signs; chaos would result. **It's** important to use the appropriate signs, and then your reader will quickly and efficiently be able to read and comprehend your document. Don't you find it rather difficult reading this exercise with no punctuation marks?

36. I want a doctor who doesn't double book_____patients.
    a. his or her
    b. his

37. What qualifications does one need to be a_____?
    a. fireman
    b. firefighter

38. Alaina loves to write and dreams of becoming a famous_____.
    a. poet
    b. female poet

39. Please address this invitation to_____.
    a. Mr. and Mrs. G. Brown
    b. Eleanor and Mr. Brown
    c. Mr. and Mrs. Brown

40. Four_____ and six men sat on the discussion panel.
    a. women
    b. ladies
    c. girls

Directions: Choose the **correctly written** sentence.

41.
    a. 42 people signed up for the fitness workshop.
    b. Forty-two people signed up for the fitness workshop.

42.

    a. **The three catering trucks will arrive at 12 noon.**

    b. The 3 catering trucks will arrive at 12 p.m.

43.

    a. Tomorrow, 150 high school seniors, five mentors and 13 coaches will arrive.

    b. **Tomorrow, 150 high school seniors, 5 mentors and 13 coaches will arrive.**

44.

    a. One communications textbook costs $225.00.

    b. **One communications textbook costs $225.**

Directions: Make all necessary **changes** to expressions of **numbers**.

---

45. Yesterday, my administrative assistant contacted the Joe C. Thompson Conference Center at 4455 **Third** Street in Austin to determine whether it had suitable space available for July **10-13**. She indicated that they had a meeting room **150 by 50 feet** that is available. There is also no restriction on time limit for use of the room if we conclude the hearings by **7 p.m.** each day.

Directions: Correct the **capitalization**, **punctuation** (e.g. commas, apostrophes, quotation marks) and **spelling errors** in the sentences below.

---

46. Please **send** copies of the report before next **Thursday**.

47. Alexander **Pope** wrote**,** "To err is human, to forgive divine."

48. Martha's manager**,** a **great** guy**,** is retiring next year.

49. You should head **north** when you reach the **town hall**.

50. **Immediately,** the fire department was called to the scene.

References

Anderson, A. (2018). Annie Oakley. Retrieved August 22, 2020, from
    https://www.womenshistory.org/education-resources/biographies/annie-oakley

Associated Press. *The Associated Press Stylebook 2017*. 52nd Edition. New
    York: Basic Books. 2017. Print.

Biography: Frank Butler. (n.d.). Retrieved August 22, 2020, from
    https://www.pbs.org/wgbh/americanexperience/features/oakley-butler/

Fawcett, S. (2011). *Evergreen: A Guide to Writing With Readings*. Boston, MA: Wadsworth.

Hampton, A. R. (2020). *Creative Business Writing*. Morrisville, N.C.: Lulu Press.

Hampton, A. R. *Grammar Essentials for Proofreading, Copyediting & Business Writing*.
    Arkansas: Cornerstone Communications & Publishing. 2018. Print.

Hampton, A. R. (2019, October 29). John Bush (1856–1916). Retrieved August 22, 2020, from
    https://encyclopediaofarkansas.net/entries/john-bush-1608

Hampton, A. R. (2019). *Proofreading Power: Skills & Drills*. Little Rock, AR: Published by
    Cornerstone Communications & Publishing.

John Bush. (2019, April 30). Retrieved August 22, 2020, from
    https://encyclopediaofarkansas.net/media/john-bush-6082/

Merriam-Webster. (n.d.). *Merriam-Webster* dictionary. Retrieved August 25, 2020, from
    https://www.merriam-webster.com/

Sabin, W. A. *The Gregg Reference Manual*. 11th Edition. New York: McGraw-Hill, 2011.

Error Hint List

How many actual errors are there in the everyday proofreading and business document exercises?

Exercise	# of Errors
EP #1	8
EP #2	13
EP #3	5
EP #4	10
EP #5	4
EP #6	7
EP #7	8
EP #8	11
EP #9	9
EP #10	22
EP #11	9
EP #12	7
EP #13	17
EP #14	8
EP #15	3
EP #16	7
BD: Agenda	7
BD: Biography	15
BD: Blog Article	14
BD: Briefing Notes	15
BD: Cover Letter	6
BD: Résumé	8
BD: Email	14
BD: Business Letter	12
BD: Sales Letter	1
BD: Press Release	14

Index